How To Delegate

Robert

D0668866

DORLING KINDERSLEY

London • New York • Sydney • Moscow

A DORLING KINDERSLEY BOOK

Project Editor Michael Downey
Project Art Editor Ian Midson
Editors Felicity Crowe, Nicola Munro
Designer Laura Watson

DTP Designer Jason Little
Production Controllers Silvia La Greca,
Michelle Thomas

Series Editor Jane Simmonds
Series Art Editor Tracy Hambleton-Miles

Managing Editor Stephanie Jackson
Managing Art Editor Nigel Duffield

First published in Great Britain in 1998
by Dorling Kindersley Limited,
9 Henrietta Street,
London WC2E 8PS

2 4 6 8 10 9 7 5 3

Copyright © 1998
Dorling Kindersley Limited, London
Text copyright © 1998 Robert Heller

Visit us on the World Wide Web at
http://www.dk.com

A CIP catalogue record for this book is available
from the British Library

ISBN 0 7513 0632 0

Reproduced by Colourscan, Singapore
Printed and bound in Italy by Graphicom srl

CONTENTS

MONITORING
PROGRESS

IMPROVING
SKILLS

INTRODUCTION

Delegation is an essential element of any manager's job. Used effectively it provides real benefits for everyone involved. How to Delegate will enable you to achieve the best possible results from each delegation you make – from small everyday tasks to major leadership appointments. The book covers every aspect of this process, from deciding and prioritizing which tasks to delegate and choosing the right person for the job, to recognizing and overcoming barriers and anticipating risks. Practical advice on how to motivate and develop staff, build loyalty, and give and receive feedback will increase your confidence and help you to become a skilled and trusted delegator. Included are 101 practical tips that summarize key points, and a self-assessment exercise that provides an insight into your performance as a delegator.

UNDERSTANDING DELEGATION

Effective delegation is an essential managerial skill.
To achieve the best results, you must be aware of its benefits
and recognize the barriers that can hinder its success.

DEFINING DELEGATION

As organizations grow increasingly complex, duties and responsibilities across the workforce can become less well defined. Often it seems as though everyone is doing everyone else's job. Delegation is the manager's key to efficiency, and benefits all.

1 Use delegation to benefit you, your staff, and your organization.

▲ **DELEGATING FOR MANAGERIAL SUCCESS**
An effective manager must monitor a delegated project, assuming responsibility while allowing the delegate autonomy.

EXPLAINING DELEGATION
Delegation involves entrusting another person with a task for which the delegator remains ultimately responsible. Delegation can range from a major appointment, such as the leadership of a team developing a new product, to one of any number of smaller tasks in the everyday life of any organization – from arranging an annual outing to interviewing a job candidate. Examining the overall structure of an organization will reveal a complex web of delegated authority, usually in the form of management chains, providing a mechanism for reporting and control.

EXPLORING THE FUNDAMENTALS

The basic issues involved in delegation are autonomy and control. How much authority is the delegate able to exercise without referring back to the delegator? How far should the delegator exercise direct influence over the work of the delegate? When choosing a delegate, you are assessing whether a particular person is fully capable of performing the task within available resources. Having appointed a delegate, you must ensure that they are allowed sufficient autonomy to undertake the task in their own way, subject to an initial briefing and regular reports on progress.

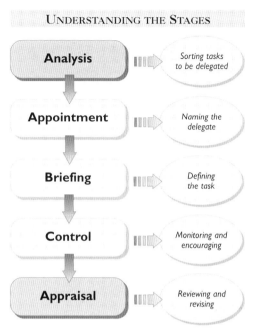

UNDERSTANDING THE STAGES

Analysis ▷ Sorting tasks to be delegated

Appointment ▷ Naming the delegate

Briefing ▷ Defining the task

Control ▷ Monitoring and encouraging

Appraisal ▷ Reviewing and revising

DEFINING THE PROCESS

The unending process of delegation is integral to the manager's role. The process begins with the analysis – selecting the tasks that the manager could, and should, delegate. When the tasks are selected, the parameters of each should be clearly defined. This will help the delegator to appoint an appropriate delegate and to provide as accurate a brief as possible. Whatever the role, proper briefing is essential – you cannot hold people responsible for vague or undefined tasks. Monitoring of some kind is also essential, but should be used for control and coaching rather than interference. The final stage is appraisal. How well has the delegate performed? What changes, on both sides, need to be made to improve performance?

2 Always be positive when reviewing – expect to hear good news.

3 Show faith in your chosen delegate, even if others have reservations.

WHY DELEGATE?

Delegation has a number of benefits. When you streamline your workload, you increase the amount of time available for essential managerial tasks. Your staff feel motivated and more confident, and stress levels decrease across the workforce.

4 Delegate to boost staff morale, build confidence, and reduce stress.

INCREASING YOUR TIME

Managers commonly claim that the short-term demands of operational and minor duties make it impossible to devote sufficient time to more important, long-term matters. Strategic planning, control, and training are among the higher level activities which will suffer under the burden of undelegated, routine tasks which you wrongly attempt to do yourself. To create more time for yourself, more routine work must be handed down by delegation. Also, the more frequently you delegate the more experienced staff become, and the less time you need to spend on briefing.

5 Set aside enough time each day for concentrating on your long-term projects.

REDUCING STRESS

The pressure on managers to perform under demanding conditions can lead to a marked increase in stress levels. The symptoms are visible in erratic and sometimes disorientated personal behaviour, mounting paperwork on desks, and overcrowded diaries. Clearing your desk, and your diary, is best accomplished through delegation. Fully effective delegation not only eases the pressure on the delegator, but can benefit the delegate and the team or department as a whole. Before delegating, consider carefully the task requirements, and make a realistic assessment of your proposed delegate's abilities.

QUESTIONS TO ASK YOURSELF

Q Am I devoting enough time and resources to strategic planning and overall monitoring?

Q Is my desk overflowing with uncompleted tasks?

Q Are staff enthusiastic and sufficiently motivated?

Q Am I delegating routine but necessary tasks to staff?

Q Is staff training given priority to ensure effective skills for future delegation plans?

DELEGATING TO MOTIVATE

A sense of achievement is central to any employee's job satisfaction. Effective delegation involves the stimulus of increased responsibility and can provide a delegate with an enriched level of satisfaction as well as a greater sense of worth. Delegation is empowerment, and that is the mainspring of better work. Your staff will not develop unless they are given tasks that build their abilities, experience, and confidence. They will perform best in a structured environment in which everyone is aware of delegated duties and responsibilities and has the necessary skills and resources to carry out tasks efficiently. Use regular and effective feedback sessions as tools for maintaining a delegate's motivation.

6 Make sure you have the right experience to coach others.

7 If delegation is not working, ask yourself, "What am I doing wrong?"

THE COSTS OF AVOIDING DELEGATION

Delegation takes time to organize and prioritize but the costs of avoiding it are high. The manager who does not delegate or delegates inefficiently will not only seem disorganized, but will spend many hours each week completing low-priority tasks. This can result in excessive hours worked by senior managers, low morale among under-employed staff, basic processes slowed down by bottlenecks, poor quality of work, and missed deadlines. Together, all of these factors will have a detrimental effect on long-term performance.

▼ **DELEGATING INEFFECTIVELY**
A manager who avoids delegation cannot possibly hope to complete effectively all of the tasks that find their way on to his or her desk.

RECOGNIZING AND DEALING WITH BARRIERS

Managers can find delegation difficult. Barriers preventing delegation are often based on negative feelings of insecurity and mistrust. The gains achieved through overcoming these feelings and beginning to trust will far outweigh any possible losses.

8 Avoid keeping work because you do it better – that is bad management.

DOING IT YOURSELF

As a manager, you will probably be more efficient at many tasks than your staff. But if you attempt to do everything because you are quicker, surer, and more proficient you will inevitably find yourself overburdened. As a result you will not have sufficient time to spend on the higher-level tasks that only you can do. Moreover, how will your staff become proficient if they are not given the opportunity to learn and perform more tasks?

MISUSE OF A ▼ MANAGER'S TIME
Here the manager is not only doing his own job, but is wasting time that should be spent on more important work by performing the routine, non-managerial tasks that could and should be delegated to appropriate subordinates.

Manager works on appropriate, high-level task

Menial tasks waste time and energy

Faxing does not need to be done by a manager

OVERBURDENING STAFF

The fear of overburdening staff is a strong barrier to delegation – it is natural for conscientious managers to want to ensure that staff workloads are not excessive. If staff members appear to be working to full capacity, how can you delegate tasks without overburdening them? One solution is to keep back tasks and find time to do them yourself. A more sensible approach is to make employees analyze their own use of time and free capacity for more work. If staff shortage is truly the problem, the answer is to take on more staff. It is important not to allow the overburdening argument to result in overwork for yourself.

Q How much of my time is spent on things that I should be delegating to colleagues?

Q Can I learn from the way my own boss delegates to me?

Q Have I got my paperwork under control?

Q Why should it upset me if a subordinate performs part of my job brilliantly?

Q How much spare work capacity is there in my unit?

9 Delegate efficiently to strengthen your own performance.

10 Be loyal to your staff and they will be loyal to you.

BEING INEXPERIENCED

The basic mechanics of the delegation process involve common management skills that delegators should develop, including skills in controlling and reviewing. The challenge for managers with limited experience of delegation is to master the more complex aspects of the process, such as attaining an effective and appropriate leadership style. Delegation is a self-teaching activity – you develop and perfect skills through the process itself, and your confidence and abilities increase the more you delegate.

LOSING CONTROL OF TASKS

The desire to be in total control is a common human trait. Delegation involves the loss of direct control, and this loss is a potential barrier to the delegation process. When delegating, the manager passes on responsibility for completion of a task to a chosen delegate. The delegator, however, retains overall control by appointing the right person, having a clear idea of how the task should progress, and exchanging regular feedback.

11 Expect delegated performance at least to equal your own standards.

DEALING WITH FEAR

Fear is a major barrier to delegation. Sometimes managers fear that delegates will perform so well that they challenge the delegator's own position. A parallel fear is that "losing" part of the job diminishes personal importance. These fears may underlie a third – that the delegate will do badly. Tackle the fears by asking yourself four questions: Is the task suitable for delegation? Is the delegate competent to perform the task? Will I brief them fully and correctly? Will I give them all the right backup, authority, and resources? If the answers are positive, then there is nothing to fear, and the delegation should succeed.

POINTS TO REMEMBER

- Possessive feelings about work are negative and unproductive.
- Keeping hold of minor tasks impedes the development of effective management.
- Analysis of staff work time is sure to reveal spare capacity.
- It is self-defeating and wastes time to attempt to manage without the use of schedules.
- Delegation involves the loss of direct control but the retention of overall responsibility.

12 Encourage people who claim to be overworked to keep a time log.

FEELING INSECURE

Insecure managers who do not take advantage of delegation underuse employees and actually endanger their own security. But if you enlist skilled and motivated people to carry out the delegated work, there is no need to feel insecure. The use of delegation, far from being a threat to a delegator's position at work, actually enhances performance and therefore increases job security. That is why many top managers have remarkably clear desks – they concentrate on a small number of priority tasks, and delegate everything else.

BEING SUSPICIOUS

Managers can still be unsure even when their staff have proved their competence. The bad delegator believes that a job, particularly one that is important, must be done "their way". This leads to very restrictive briefings that give the delegate little space for initiative. Resist any urge you may have to interfere more than necessary, as this will only create more work and worry for you, thus defeating the object of the delegation.

13 Remember that letting go of work gets easier the more you do it.

14 Use the delegation of tasks as an effective means of training your staff.

15 If you often say "I don't have enough time", you are badly organized.

BEING TOO BUSY

Planning your own daily and weekly schedule is an essential precondition of effective delegation. An overworked manager, with a disorganized and overloaded schedule, is both the villain and the victim of inadequate delegation. It is all too easy to establish a vicious circle. You do not delegate enough because you lack the time to explain or monitor the tasks which should be delegated, therefore you are always busy doing the tasks that should have been delegated – which means that you lack the time to explain or monitor the tasks which should be delegated, and so on. Organize your schedule to ensure that you have enough time available to plan and manage a delegation properly, including writing an effective brief and the actual monitoring of your delegates.

LACKING TRUST

If both sides in the delegation process do not trust each other, the process will be hindered. A manager must have complete confidence in a delegate's ability to perform the task, and delegates should feel that their managers are consistent and fair in their approach. Subordinates must feel assured about their manager's integrity, competence, and loyalty. On both sides, the trust is conditional. Trust is not blind and its continuation depends on good performance. Maintain trust by showing respect to your delegate and by giving honest and constructive feedback during the delegation.

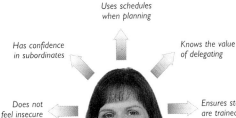

Uses schedules when planning

Has confidence in subordinates

Knows the value of delegating

Does not feel insecure

Ensures staff are trained

THE EFFECTIVE DELEGATOR

▲ OVERCOMING BARRIERS

When you recognize the barriers that are preventing you from delegating effectively, you are more than halfway towards dealing with them. Once you have overcome your initial fears, your efficiency as a delegator and manager will be greatly increased.

BUILDING A RELATIONSHIP

Frankness, openness, and effective communication are essential to successful delegation, helping to build and sustain trust and overcome many personal barriers. You can reinforce trust and nurture mutual esteem through careful management.

16 Make sure you give people plenty of authority rather than too little.

COMMUNICATING WELL

When managers keep knowledge to themselves, communicate sporadically and incompletely, or even make no attempt to tell the truth at all, mistrust and other negative feelings in their staff will build rapidly. But misunderstandings and unjustified suspicions can result even when people believe they are discussing matters openly and honestly. Some managers hear only what they want to hear, and employees may be afraid to contradict them. To be a good communicator, you must express your ideas clearly and develop your listening skills. This will encourage others to share their thoughts and opinions with you.

17 Always deal swiftly and positively with idle and unjustified rumours.

COMPARING PERCEPTIONS

When assessing whether you are a helpful and accomplished delegator, you must always bear in mind the delegate's point of view. You may uncover a surprising gulf in the way a situation is perceived. Make it clear from the start that you want and expect honest opinions about your delegating style. If the feedback you receive indicates that you are thought of as interfering and distrustful, act immediately to correct the situation. The more delegates realize that they have real responsibility and will not be second-guessed, the better they will do.

18 If you do not trust a member of staff, do not keep them.

19 Treat your own perceptions as facts and analyze them objectively.

RESPECTING OPINIONS

Treat everyone with the same respect that you expect yourself, because your staff are allies in the job of management. When you delegate, you show respect by entrusting part of your work to another because you believe in their capability and their suitability. To build mutual respect, ask your delegates for their opinions on how the work should be done, and show you are listening to their suggestions.

DO'S AND DON'TS

☑ Do use all means to communicate with your staff.

☑ Do strive to regard your associates as competent people.

☑ Do remind delegates that you respect and appreciate them.

☑ Do show your delegates loyalty and support.

☑ Do allow delegates the opportunity to give their opinions.

☒ Don't be dismayed by differing perceptions – they are natural.

☒ Don't forget that trust is a two-way process that can take time and effort to establish.

☒ Don't ask people to do things that you wouldn't do yourself.

☒ Don't use delegates as scapegoats when things go wrong.

☒ Don't dissuade staff from speaking out.

LOOKING AT TRANSACTIONAL ANALYSIS

Understanding how people behave with each other helps build successful delegating relationships. Transactional Analysis is a systematic approach to interpersonal behaviour that defines three "ego" systems:

● PARENT: Directive, rigid, controlling, supportive.
● ADULT: Rational, objective, fact orientated.
● CHILD: Self-centred, dependent, stubborn.

By observation it is possible to recognize which system is dominant in an individual. For example, people may dominate others by using their PARENT mode to provoke the other's CHILD. Or the CHILD may take a "poor me" stance to control others. Productive delegation depends on mutual trust and respect, and Transactional Analysis suggests that this is best achieved if the ADULT system is most active.

USING THE RIGHT ATTITUDE ▶
The interpersonal process of delegation is greatly enhanced if relationships are conducted in an honest and open ADULT to ADULT way.

DELEGATING EFFECTIVELY

The most successful delegators are expert, self-disciplined managers who are efficient at choosing tasks to delegate and able to monitor and provide positive feedback to each delegate.

SELECTING TASKS

Before you can improve your delegating technique you must decide which tasks you could, or should, be delegating. The selection process involves assessing your time and that of your subordinates, and grouping and prioritizing activities.

20 Do not allow people to create unnecessary work for you.

21 Review and revise your detailed time log every three to six months.

ANALYZING YOUR TIME

The way you, as a manager, distribute your work and how much time you allocate is probably under your control. A useful exercise is to determine how your actual expenditure of time matches the areas or tasks for which you are responsible. Start the analysis by keeping a detailed time log for at least two weeks: note all activities you undertake and the time they take. You will probably find that only a small amount of your time has been spent on the high-level activities that only you can do. Far more time will have been taken up by routine activities that could have been delegated.

BREAKING DOWN YOUR TASKS

After analyzing your use of time, analyze the tasks you are undertaking. Do this by dividing the tasks listed in your time log into the three groups outlined by the management writer Peter Drucker: those that do not need to be done at all – by you or anyone else; those that you could and should delegate; and those that you are not able to delegate and must do yourself. Use this breakdown as a basis for reducing any unnecessary activities, delegating more tasks, and concentrating on tasks that only you can complete.

EVALUATING YOUR ACTIVITIES

What tasks am I doing that need not be done at all? → *Do not complete them yourself or delegate them*

What am I doing that could be done by someone else? → *Delegate these tasks to subordinates*

What tasks am I doing that can only be done by me? → *You cannot delegate these, so prioritize them*

CONSIDERING OTHER IMPORTANT FACTORS

When you come to choose which tasks to delegate, there are several points that you must consider. Some of the most important of those factors are:

● That unnecessary activities are eliminated from the task list altogether;

● That you are able to concentrate your attention on the tasks that only you can do;

● That there are enough suitably qualified delegates for the tasks to be delegated;

● That, where necessary, the delegation has been cleared with your own superior.

Obviously, these are not the only points you need to think about, but once you have considered and acted upon them – along with any others that you think are important – you can move on to the next stage of the delegating process: prioritizing.

22 If possible, attend only the meetings directly relevant to your work.

23 If you cannot fix a meeting for weeks ahead, you are not delegating enough.

PRIORITIZING TASKS

Having decided which tasks to delegate, your first concern is to allocate these tasks. Then prioritize the tasks you have decided to handle yourself according to their importance or urgency. Start each day by listing these tasks and tackle them one by one in order of priority. If circumstances allow, always complete a task before starting a new one. The closer you keep to this system, the more effective you will be.

24 Do not prioritize easy tasks over those that are more arduous.

ESTIMATING TIME

When delegating tasks you need to have a fairly accurate idea of how long each task will take to complete. Base this estimate either on your own experience or the experience of others. Try not to tie your delegates to an excessively tight schedule, but always encourage them to improve their own time management and the time spent on a task. This approach is essential and invariably effective. You and they will find that the time spent on tasks – especially routines that go unchallenged for years – can often be greatly shortened by cutting out any unnecessary stages, or by radically changing processes and working methods.

25 Do not attempt to undertake more than seven tasks in one day.

GROUPING TASKS

Your list of tasks to be done – either by yourself or a delegate – will produce activities that are related to, or have affinities with, each other. Study these carefully and group them under specific headings: administration, human resources, or financial, for example. You can then consider delegating each group of related tasks to one person. More importantly, if you have a potential delegate who particularly enjoys and is good at administrative tasks, say, it makes perfect sense for that person to deal with all of them.

26 Make a habit of challenging long-standing routines.

MAKING CHOICES

Ultimately, the choice of what you delegate, however logical the analysis has been, will have an element of subjectivity. Some jobs that could be delegated will be especially dear to you. For example, you may choose to retain close day-to-day contact with certain suppliers that you have known for a long time – suppliers that could be dealt with by a subordinate. Provided these tasks have no adverse impact on general effectiveness, this is perfectly acceptable. However, do not allow your choice to be dictated by dislikes – you cannot always delegate the tasks you do not like. So periodically revise the list of activities only you can do and consider whether the list could be cut down, perhaps by training somebody to do a task.

POINTS TO REMEMBER

- Tasks should be listed in order of priority based on their urgency and importance.
- Undertaking work that you cannot carry out shows willing but is counter-productive.
- Every moment of your day should be used efficiently, and time-wasting should be eliminated from your schedule.
- Responsibility for an entire task should be given to one employee whenever possible.
- New opportunities for the delegation of tasks should be sought continuously.

AN EXAMPLE OF TASK GROUPING

THE PROJECT

THE DELEGATOR
A senior employee is asked to organize the manufacture and launch of a new product. While retaining overall responsibility, he decides to list what needs doing and group the work into three key areas for delegation.

THE TASKS TO BE DELEGATED

STAFF RECRUITMENT
The delegator asks one person to produce a human resources strategy that will supply multi-skilled staff in advance of deadlines and will operate within the agreed financial constraints.

PRODUCT MANUFACTURE
He asks another person to produce a work flow chart, a layout of the manufacturing process, a programme to meet deadlines, and details of the quality assurance procedures.

MARKETING
He asks a third person to calculate a budget to cover the total costs of marketing the new product to both established and new customers, including mailings and sales trips.

DECIDING WHICH TASKS TO KEEP

As a manager you should delegate as many of the lower-level operational tasks as possible. But you cannot delegate such areas as, for example, strategic planning, occasional crisis management, and sensitive matters such as salaries and promotion.

27 Always be aware of those tasks that you absolutely cannot delegate.

28 Plan your thinking time as a meeting, with an agenda and timetable.

RETAINING TASKS

Tasks that you cannot delegate include key areas such as controlling overall performance, and confidential human resources matters – how people are rewarded, appraised, promoted, informed, coached, and counselled. You may also need to manage all dealings with important customers. Make these tasks your priority and ensure that you allocate ample time to them.

SETTING ASIDE THINKING TIME

Tasks that you cannot delegate have common themes – meeting the strategic objectives of the organization, the team, and you the manager. Typically, a manager is immersed in operational detail, such as gathering information or organizing meetings, and spends only 20 per cent of the working week in high-level thinking. By delegating effectively you can reorganize your time to allow strategic planning, or thinking, to occupy the largest segment of your time. Delegation and effective use of information technology could treble the time available for thinking to about 60 per cent of the working week.

| 20% thinking | 80% other tasks |
| 60% thinking | 40% other tasks |

AVERAGE WEEK   IDEAL WEEK

TASKS MANAGERS SHOULD RETAIN

RESPONSIBILITIES	FACTORS TO CONSIDER
LEADERSHIP Providing the drive and stewardship for a project or an organization.	A leadership task is one that is essential for leading a group or project to success. Because of its importance to control, it cannot usually be delegated to a subordinate but can be shared with one or two senior colleagues.
REWARD Setting and maintaining parameters for salaries and bonus schemes.	The setting of general and individual levels of pay and other remuneration is so basic to motivation that it clearly falls within the manager's remit. The same is true of any significant non-financial rewards.
CONTROL Achieving optimum performance in the working environment.	Day-to-day working discipline, accurate systems, quality procedures, and efficient execution do not have to be the manager's operational tasks. But the responsibility for seeing that controls are effective cannot be delegated.
PERSONNEL Controlling human resource matters, conduct, and discipline.	The manager must take a close interest in staff careers and performance, personally conducting reviews and appraisals and taking sensitive and confidential decisions on promotions, reviews, hirings, and dismissals.
KEY CUSTOMERS Maintaining key relationships that rely on personal and social skills.	The continued success of a business is closely tied to continued good relationships with key customers. The manager must never endanger these relationships by delegating ultimate responsibility for these contacts.
STRATEGY Establishing key targets and the means of fulfilling them.	Planning for the future (short-, medium-, and long-term) is a task that must be originated and led from the top, but which depends for full success on enlisting committed contributions from all levels of the team.
COMMUNICATIONS Ensuring the efficient internal transfer of information.	Making sure that good channels of communication exist and are used continuously cannot be delegated. The manager ensures that on both a personal and group level, a smooth flow of relevant information is maintained.
RESULTS Assessing outcomes and the application of lessons learned.	The manager sets the goals, in agreement with all staff, and monitors the successful progress towards these goals. When any targets are endangered, the manager steps in and immediately acts to improve the situation.

Planning a Structure with Delegation

Delegation is a planned and organized sharing of responsibility that requires careful structuring. Once you have decided which tasks to delegate and which to keep, set up a structure and devise an overall plan for all the individual delegations involved.

29 Devote sufficient time and effort to the organizational plan and structure.

30 Cultivate trouble-shooting talents for emergency delegations.

Planning a Structure

A planned delegation on any scale, from a few individuals to an entire company, provides the basis for a structure that resembles a set of building blocks, each representing a specific responsibility, and each with a specific person in charge. The stability of the whole structure depends on the individual blocks: remove any and the edifice may tumble down. For added stability, ensure that delegated tasks are directly relevant to the delegate's overall job responsibility, and that every delegate has a direct reporting line to the delegator.

▼ USING A FAULTY STRUCTURE
An organizational structure in which any key part is missing, or the whole is badly planned, is a weak and unstable edifice liable to collapse in times of crisis.

DISTRIBUTION

SALES

MARKETING

MANUFACTURE

MAINTENANCE

ADMINISTRATION

FINANCE

TECHNICAL SUPPORT

SETTING UP A STRUCTURE

When setting up a structure, your priority will be to ensure that the organizational framework is balanced and responsive to any of the inevitable changes that can occur. Do this by ensuring that each delegate has sufficient support and back-up when unforeseen problems arise and that, as far as possible, adequate cover will always be made available in any absence. Inform each delegate of the support structure you have devised so that each knows where they can go to seek assistance immediately in a crisis. When planning the structure, remember that it is your responsibility as the delegator to ensure that the structure remains relevant, stable, and effective.

THINGS TO DO

1. Draw up a delegation plan.
2. Inform delegates of your plans well in advance.
3. Consider the overall structure when delegating.
4. Ensure that delegates know to whom they are reporting.
5. Monitor the progress of each task to make sure that no gaps or overlaps appear.

AVOIDING DUPLICATION

When planning a structure, delegating, and distributing tasks, avoid giving the same task to more than one person or overlooking a task so that it is not done at all. To prevent confusion, create a chart with all key activities listed on the left-hand side, and the names of those with delegated responsibility along the bottom line. Tick off each box in the chart with both a task and a delegate to reveal any gaps or overlaps in the distribution and structure of the tasks.

31 Start considering possible delegates when planning the tasks to be done.

DELEGATING IN ADVANCE

It is inappropriate to treat delegation as simply a way for a harassed manager to shed excessive work during busy periods. As the start date of a project for which you are responsible draws near, plan and make any delegated appointments as early as possible. This will give you sufficient time to prepare a detailed brief, and will allow you and your delegate to discuss task requirements fully and arrange any training that may be needed.

32 Ensure you provide enough support and back-up to each delegate.

CONSIDERING ROLES

Unless you are intending to delegate the management of an entire project, you will need to consider the various roles that could be delegated. Assess these in relation to potential team members and consider the contribution each individual could make.

> **33** Ensure that you have an informed assessment of a delegate's abilities.

DEFINING THE TASKS

To delegate effectively, you need to define the tasks and also have a good understanding of a proposed delegate's abilities. So for each task in your planned delegation, work out a clear definition, including the skills required and the range of responsibilities to be delegated. Go through this process whether you are delegating a large project with a number of constituent parts requiring different skills, or a simple, one-off task.

> **34** Be supportive of all delegates whenever any mistakes are made.

TRAINING DELEGATES

When you are planning delegations in advance, consider which skills will need to be taught or developed to enable the potential delegates to undertake tasks successfully. Remember that even a skilled and highly experienced delegate may well require help in mastering a new role. Specific training will not only provide delegates with invaluable knowledge about the task they are to be involved with, but will also complement their other abilities. Additionally, teaching will motivate the delegate and strengthen their self-confidence.

> **35** Do not give advice if delegates can manage without it.

▼ **DEVELOPING STAFF**
Training serves two purposes: strengthening skills needed in new roles, and motivating staff as they become more competent.

Teach ➤ **Strengthen** ➤ **Motivate**

ASSESSING INDIVIDUALS

Having clearly defined the tasks involved, carefully consider the qualities of all members of your team and begin thinking about which roles may suit each individual, bearing in mind their strengths and weaknesses. For example, when assessing the role of cost controller for a project, the manager will be looking for a delegate with good numerical skills and sufficient self-confidence to initiate any cost-cutting measures that may prove necessary.

36 Pick delegates who are honest enough to tell you if they disagree with you.

LOOKING FOR INITIATIVE

Initiative is an ideal quality in any potential delegate, so look at your team to see who acts on their own initiative, and bear them in mind for more responsible and challenging roles. Remember that a person who has strong ideas and opinions of their own may sometimes disagree with their manager. An employee who is prepared to do this is showing self-confidence – a desirable quality that should be encouraged. Disagreement is not insubordination, and must not be treated as such.

ENCOURAGING ▼
INITIATIVE
Here the manager appreciates the initiative the delegate has shown in preparing in advance all he needs to put his ideas across as clearly as possible.

A confident approach to the manager

The manager is impressed by the delegate's approach

Delegate presents ideas clearly

UNDERSTANDING ACCOUNTABILITY

Accountability is at the very heart of delegation, so before you finally select your delegates consider who you are going to make responsible for what. Accountability must be strictly defined so that there is no doubt over where it lies and what it covers.

37 Make clear to delegates the areas for which they are accountable.

SETTING GUIDELINES

Delegation operates within guidelines, and the most important of these is an understanding that each delegate will be accountable for a specific task. It follows that you must define the task very clearly, and the delegate must confirm that they fully understand what the task involves. However clear the delegation, and however much you wish to avoid interference, there are likely be occasions when the delegate does not know what to do. The guideline here is: when really in doubt, ask.

38 Always confirm all paths of accountability in written form.

AVOIDING OVERLAPS

To avoid any confusion over which delegate is accountable for what part of a task, break down delegated tasks into specific elements and allocate each element to a named person. Within the overall structure of responsibility, make each delegate accountable for his or her own particular component of the task – for example, controlling expenditure or processing contracts with outside suppliers. This "single-point accountability" is not only very precise, it will also greatly reduce the risk of you giving more than one delegate responsibility for the same task or part of a task.

39 Encourage staff with shared tasks to form effective partnerships.

SHARING ACCOUNTABILITY

In general, delegation is most effective when accountability for a task rests with one individual. This avoids confusion and the tendency for one party to blame another for a mistake or failure. A pooling of accountability, however, is natural in self-managed teams or project groups where leadership is shared by the members. In these groups all decisions relating to a project are reached through collective effort, and all team members are jointly accountable for the outcome of their work: that is one of the basic strengths of teamwork. For shared accountability to work effectively, it should follow the same principles as for individual accountability – a clear and agreed definition and breakdown of tasks into very precise, individually allocated "single-point" elements to eliminate any possible overlaps.

40 Establish a culture that recognizes success and avoids blame for failure.

41 Ensure that written documents are circulated to all relevant staff.

▲ **INDIVIDUAL ACCOUNTABILITY**
Each member of this four-person sales and marketing team is individually accountable to a sales director for a specific area. The director plans strategy and has responsibility for the performance of the team.

▲ **SHARED ACCOUNTABILITY**
In this self-managed sales team each member shares equal responsibility for planning and implementing a strategy for the unit, for the attainment of targets within a set budget, and for the team's efficiency.

CHOOSING THE RIGHT PERSON

It is very important to choose the right person for the task in hand. The first few times, it will be a case of trial and error, but before long you should learn how better to assess the skills, and therefore the person, needed for every situation that arises.

42 Never accept a delegate's own self-deprecating assessment.

43 Be sure that you are always available should a delegate require help on a given project.

MAKING QUICK DECISIONS

If a job must be completed in a hurry and you can resist the impulse to do it yourself, you may be tempted to commandeer the nearest available person. Occasionally these sudden demands can reveal unsuspected talents, but sometimes not – with negative consequences. If circumstances force you to make a quick decision and you have any choice at all, pick the person whose overall experience is most relevant. Bear in mind that the monitoring will have to be closer than usual.

BEING OBJECTIVE

For more considered, structured delegation, it is important that your assessment of a person's suitability for a particular task is not clouded by irrational factors. For example, a predecessor or colleague may have influenced you by making an erroneous judgment based on prejudice, or you yourself may have gained a negative impression of somebody based on a single unrepresentative incident. To ensure that you make your decision fairly and objectively, always use your written job definition to match the candidate's skills and abilities to the requirements of the task.

CULTURAL DIFFERENCES

In countries such as the US, with strong hire-and-fire cultures, managers delegate more freely than those in Japan, who are likely to be highly selective since failure is considered shameful. In highly structured cultures, like Germany, managers retain more control of tasks, delegating less.

EVALUATING STAFF

Choosing the right person for a task requires careful assessment of experience and specific abilities. Different types of tasks require different skills. For example, a job may demand speed over accuracy, or vice versa. The ideal candidate for a specific delegation may not exist – in which case, your choice will necessarily involve an element of compromise. Remember that a delegation can be used to train and develop a valued employee's range and depth of skills with a view to future promotion.

44 Ensure that staff do not take on too much work.

COMPARING STAFF ATTRIBUTES

POSITIVE	NEGATIVE
● Mary is analytical in her approach and can get to the root of a problem quickly. ● She has a great grasp of the details of a task.	● Mary cannot handle the pressure of urgent deadlines. ● It often takes her some time to grasp the whole picture.
● Gordon is capable of tackling most delegated tasks with confidence. ● He is an excellent and willing all-rounder.	● Gordon tends to delegate too few tasks himself. ● He finds it hard to apply himself to a long-term project.
● Jane is good at organizing schedules and budgets. ● She is an enthusiastic and co-operative team player.	● Jane does not show enough initiative. ● She is not confident when working without supervision.

TRAINING STAFF

If you cannot find enough suitably experienced or qualified staff, and new hirings are ruled out, the soft option is not to delegate at all. That choice is negative and self-defeating. It reflects failure to provide enough continuous staff training and development to fill identified future needs. Good training enables you to build people's capability, which will often have remarkable results. The more skills each member of staff has, the greater your choice of potential delegates. Training also has beneficial effects on motivation as people feel more valued when you invest in their futures.

QUESTIONS TO ASK YOURSELF

Q Is there anybody who could, and should, be doing more important work?

Q Do my staff each have at least one task that will develop and improve their skills?

Q Are all my staff multiskilled, and if not, what am I doing to make them so?

Q Am I doing anything just because nobody else can?

PREPARING A BRIEF

When planning a brief, first define your objective and compile a full checklist to ensure that all the individual aspects of a task are included. The more complete the final brief, the more confident you can be that the task will be successfully executed.

45 Make all the objectives as precise as possible when briefing.

46 Do not set too many controls when you are writing a delegate's final brief.

DEFINING THE OBJECTIVE

The most important part of the briefing process is defining the overall objective clearly. As far as possible, outline the aims in terms of required outcomes. For example, ask a delegate to "reorganize stationery purchasing by 31 March to achieve 10 per cent savings on present costs", rather than to "sort out the stationery". Here, the saving in costs could be included in the brief as a sub-objective within a broader project for improving office efficiency and administration.

USING A CHECKLIST

Your delegation should be based on breaking down a task into all aspects, naming the person who is responsible for each item, and eliminating overlaps of responsibility. This provides the basis for making a checklist. Use this list to ensure that nothing significant has been omitted from the brief, and that component tasks have an explicit timetable. If the task is to improve the efficiency of repairs carried out on a customer's premises, for example, the key factors are likely to include identifying faults and their root causes, preventing recurrence of shortcomings, speeding up response and repair times, and assessing and raising the degree of customer satisfaction. Make sure that the checklist and the brief dovetail precisely.

THINGS TO DO

1. Keep objectives as clear and concise as possible.
2. Build a certain amount of flexibility into the brief.
3. Base the objectives on required outcomes.
4. Make a checklist to avoid overlaps and omissions.
5. Ensure that the delegate is fully aware of the aims.
6. Allow the delegate to comment on the brief.

STRUCTURING A BRIEF

PARTS OF A BRIEF	FACTORS TO CONSIDER
OBJECTIVES Defines the task, listing the major objectives and sub-objectives in clear and concise language.	List all the objectives and discuss them with the delegate before finalizing any agreement. Ensure that this list is referred to continually.
RESOURCES Specifies what personnel, finance, and facilities are available or need to be obtained.	Finalize resource needs after the objectives have been set. Ensure you include the limits to spending authority in the delegate's budget.
TIMESCALE Sets out the schedule with review points, stage completion dates, and final deadlines.	Use the schedule to motivate the delegate and to provide the basis for a critical path analysis showing all the completion stages.
METHOD Describes procedures, as agreed with the delegate, and summarizes the key points.	Devise and agree a thorough outline plan that will provide the delegate with a concrete but flexible methodology within which to work.
LEVELS OF AUTHORITY Specifies the range of the delegate's authority and to whom they will report.	Apply authority limits that tell the delegate when it may be appropriate to refer to you, and when they should use their own initiative.

ALLOWING FLEXIBILITY

Do not regard your brief as sacrosanct, but as a framework within which delegates can use reasonable flexibility in order to achieve their objectives. Be very precise about what delegates are expected to achieve, what financial and other resources will be available, when the role begins and what its deadlines are, and what delegates may or may not do on their own authority. Keep the brief tightly focused on the results you want, but leave delegates as much flexibility as possible in following the brief, especially in deciding what procedures to use. You should expect them to seek review and revision of the brief as events demand.

47 Incorporate a reporting plan into each brief.

48 Ensure that the delegate fully understands and agrees to the brief.

SECURING AGREEMENT IN PRINCIPLE

Agreeing a brief in principle with your proposed delegate involves contributions from both sides. You must motivate the delegate and confirm their suitability, while the delegate has to understand the brief and consider whether they can take on the task.

49 Approach the delegate first before finalizing the brief.

USING THE RIGHT APPROACH

It is frustrating to present a final brief to a delegate only to have them raise doubts about the task. Always obtain an agreement in principle before finalizing, as the delegate's collaboration is essential if the brief is to be fully workable. Your choice of time, place, and method for negotiating with a chosen delegate can make the difference between a positive and negative response. Location is determined by the level of the appointment. For a high-level delegation, you may take the individual to lunch; for routine tasks, the office will suffice. Whatever venue you choose, approach all potential delegates with their needs in mind, encouraging questions and giving full information.

GAINING AGREEMENT

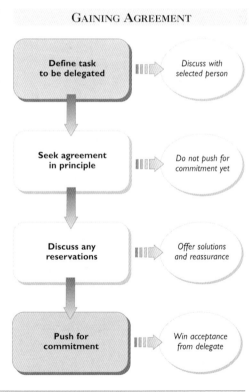

Define task to be delegated	*Discuss with selected person*
Seek agreement in principle	*Do not push for commitment yet*
Discuss any reservations	*Offer solutions and reassurance*
Push for commitment	*Win acceptance from delegate*

AIRING RESERVATIONS

If your chosen candidate is reluctant to undertake an assignment, try to discover and understand what their actual reservations are. A common objection, and a major cause of demotivation, is a perceived lack of autonomy. Do not fudge this issue, or any other areas that have given rise to objections. Give honest reassurances, and ensure that your body language reinforces your words to show confidence in the assignment and the potential delegate. By presenting the task as an opportunity to develop skills and experience further, you place the delegate in the role of a partner rather than a subordinate. If you cannot overcome the candidate's reluctance by persuasion, do not try to force acceptance. Cut your losses and look for someone else.

Manager appears confident and positive

Delegate questions certain points

DISCUSSING A BRIEF ▶
Before you finalize the brief and formally appoint a delegate, discuss its contents with your potential delegate and give him or her the opportunity to raise any reasonable reservations they may have.

50 Do not hesitate when delegating – be positive.

51 Consider positive and negative comments when finalizing the brief.

PROVIDING SUPPORT

Most people react anxiously when offered new responsibility, and many doubt their ability to perform well. To boost your chance of securing a positive response from a chosen delegate, always discuss the support, both formal and informal, that they will be able to call on during the period of delegation. Reasonable doubts can be partially dispelled by carefully considering and naming the people to whom the delegate can turn. Suggest close colleagues or staff from other departments who could provide valuable help, and discuss any training that may be appropriate. Make clear what level of support you as manager are prepared to give to ensure the delegate's success.

BRIEFING EFFECTIVELY

Once you have reached an agreement in principle, refine the brief and organize a detailed briefing meeting. Select your approach carefully, since the outcome of this meeting is vital to the success of the partnership between delegator and delegate.

52 If a delegate is negative at the briefing, reconsider the assignment.

COMMUNICATING A BRIEF

The delegator's primary task at the briefing is to communicate effectively and ensure the delegate's full understanding of the assignment. You can achieve this by adopting a methodical approach. Explain the task objective clearly and state your expectations in terms of deadlines and levels of measured achievement. List the steps that you think will have to be taken to complete the task successfully, and ask if your delegate understands. Be clear about which areas of the brief are flexible and which must be followed to the letter.

53 Keep on encouraging delegates after they have taken on a task.

SECURING AGREEMENT

Even the most carefully prepared and well-communicated brief can result in misconceptions. You can avoid misunderstandings by asking relevant questions throughout the meeting and inviting the delegate to do the same. Pay attention to body language: a lack of eye contact may indicate that your delegate is not absolutely in agreement with you, or is having trouble taking it in. If you suspect any disagreement, encourage him or her to repeat what they have heard to ensure that they understand and agree. Make it clear that you expect the delegate to use their own initiative when appropriate, and ensure that there are no doubts over the extent of their authority.

BEING BRIEFED

If you are taking on a task, the briefing session may be your only chance to discuss it in detail, so ensure that you clarify the major objectives. It is also your opportunity to discuss the allocation of resources and the flexibility of the schedule. Find out the extent of your personal autonomy, and if you feel it is inadequate, argue for more at the start – before it is too late.

SELECTING A BRIEFING METHOD

BRIEFING STYLES	FACTORS TO CONSIDER
INFORMAL "I would like you to take this on for me when you have the time."	For people you know well, and for delegating less important, simpler tasks. Verbal instruction is sufficient, although some formal follow-up may be required.
FORMAL "I have decided to put you in charge of budgetary control."	When the task is important to the group and to you. Usually accompanied by a written brief stating the task objective and how and when it should be accomplished.
COLLEGIATE "We all think you are the best person for the job."	When recognizing the particular skills of an individual within a team or taskforce, and singling them out for special responsibility. The whole group decides the brief.
LAISSEZ-FAIRE "I am not going to tell you how to do this job. I'll leave it up to you."	An ideal approach for experienced staff. You rely on your delegate to assume complete control of a task and to make key decisions without supervision or follow-up.
TROUBLE-SHOOTING "We have a problem at head office that I would like you to sort out."	A rewarding form of delegation. Your candidate is creative and is able to communicate ideas effectively. Outline the problem – he or she will know what is required.
RIGHT-HAND MAN/WOMAN "I would like you to take this off my shoulders, and improve it."	Used when you delegate part of a key task to a trusted individual whose fresh approach may provide some new solutions. You are regularly informed of progress.

ENDING A BRIEFING

Draw the briefing session to a conclusion by summarizing the key points of the delegation. End the meeting by thanking your delegate for taking on the task and communicate your confidence that the assignment will be carried out successfully – it is important to emphasize that you have appointed this delegate because you trust his or her abilities. Finally, establish a date for a follow-up meeting to review progress.

54 Ask for any new ideas when your delegate reports on task progress.

MONITORING PROGRESS

For delegation to be successful it is vital to have an effective and responsive system of controls. Use them to monitor delegates and the progress of assignments.

WORKING WITH CONTROLS

A good monitoring system consists of a light rein and a tight hand. You can always exercise more control if you feel it is necessary, but you should do so with tact and sensitivity. This is especially the case if your delegate is inexperienced.

55 Give inexperienced delegates special attention when monitoring tasks.

CULTURAL DIFFERENCES

In German-speaking countries, delegates traditionally stay under tight control at all times. Japanese delegates often have autonomy, but are expected to discuss all matters with their managers. In the UK and US the culture of delegation is encouraged but, in practice, controls can be rigid.

SUPERVISING EFFECTIVELY

The level of experience of your delegate will help you to decide whether to adopt a hands-on or hands-off approach when controlling a delegated assignment. A person with a considerable amount of experience at handling similar tasks will require less supervision and control than someone with little or no experience. But remember that the learning process has to begin somewhere, and inexperience can be overcome by good leadership. The monitoring process provides an opportunity for you to assess and extend any delegate's abilities and to supply specific skill training.

DO'S AND DON'TS

✔ Do encourage all delegates to make their own decisions.

✔ Do move from hands-on to hands-off as soon as possible.

✔ Do intervene when absolutely necessary, but only at that time.

✔ Do ask delegates if they feel thoroughly prepared for the task.

✘ Don't say or hint that you doubt the delegate's ability.

✘ Don't miss any stage in the briefing process.

✘ Don't surreptitiously take back a task.

✘ Don't place seniority above ability.

✘ Don't deny a delegate the chance to learn by interfering too much.

GUIDING A NEW DELEGATE

Assigning a task to a first-time delegate requires careful briefing and close supervision during the early stages. Help to build confidence by focusing on, and praising, good work. If an error is made, show how it could have been avoided, but try not to dwell on mistakes. You may ask an experienced colleague to help you oversee the delegate at the start of the assignment.

AVOIDING INTERFERENCE

Managers who can maintain a distance between themselves and their delegates are more likely to see positive results. Nobody will work in exactly the same way as you, so resist the temptation to intervene the moment you suspect the task is not being performed your way. Instead, set up a system of regular checks, meetings, and reports, either formal or informal, to ensure that the task objectives are being met. Heavy intervention, in which the delegator makes all the decisions, will frustrate the delegate and deny him or her the chance to gain experience. It will also save very little of the delegator's time.

DENYING AUTONOMY ▼

A manager who constantly interferes with a delegate once a task is assigned is not only denying the delegate the chance to learn new skills and gain experience, but is also not delegating effectively.

Insensitive invasion of delegate's space creates hostility

Delegate's well-ordered paperwork is needlessly disrupted

Choosing a Monitoring System

| TYPE OF SYSTEM | FACTORS TO CONSIDER |

INVOLVEMENT IN ALL CORRESPONDENCE
You retain the greatest share of authority and may expect to sign memos, invoices, and so on.

- Keeps you fully informed of developments and allows you to anticipate and avoid any bad errors of judgment.
- Could indicate that you do not trust the delegate fully.

WRITTEN REPORTS
Your delegate supplies a written commentary regarding actions, results, and any figures that are regularly updated.

- Encourages delegates to organize their thoughts clearly and give a full account of how the delegation is progressing.
- Can prove to be too remote.
- Can be used to mask problems.

PERSONAL REPORT
You arrange for the delegate to meet with you to discuss the assignment at regular intervals.

- Provides an opportunity for regular, informal updates and early airings of any potentially problematic situations.
- May encourage you to become over-involved in making decisions and taking action.

OPEN-DOOR POLICY
You encourage the delegate to bring you his or her day-to-day problems at any time for help or clarification.

- Enables you to give support and show encouragement, and stresses the collaborative aspect of delegation.
- The delegate may rely too heavily on your input, rather than use their own initiative.

ACCESS VIA COMPUTER
You use information technology systems to check directly on what is happening at any time.

- Very discreet and diplomatic and enables you to become involved only when a major decision is required.
- If used alone, may give an inaccurate or incomplete picture of the actual situation.

MEETINGS
You discuss the delegated task in a meeting which includes you, the delegate, and other staff involved in the assignment.

- Allows issues to be debated in a wider forum, and emphasizes that delegation also involves coherent teamwork.
- Can lessen the delegate's perception of personal responsibility for the task.

QUESTIONS TO ASK YOURSELF

Q Have I ensured the delegate is adequately trained?

Q Is the delegate looking at the task with a fresh eye?

Q Are too many handovers involved in delegated tasks?

Q Is the delegate delivering according to plan?

Q Are defects being picked up and corrected quickly?

Q What savings, if any, have been made by the delegate?

ELIMINATING STAGES

You can markedly reduce the amount of time spent reviewing progress by encouraging your delegates to streamline or simplify procedures. Reforming ill-conceived processes reduces the workload and cuts down on the number of stages that require monitoring. With the final objective in mind, ask delegates to work back through all the stages currently employed to the starting point of the task. With this chain of activities mapped out, look for any stages that could be combined or not done at all. In particular, ask delegates to eliminate wasteful handovers of incomplete pieces of work from one individual or department to another.

REVIEWING PROGRESS

Once a task is underway, you will need to review its progress and the performance of the delegate. There are a number of ways in which you can keep tabs on proceedings, including face-to-face discussions with the delegate, written reports, and personal observations. Choose a system that suits you, is appropriate to the task, and gives you all the information you need to review what has been achieved so far. It must also enable you to check that you are on course to achieve the objective and pinpoint any corrective action that may be required.

56 Operate on the assumption that every process can be improved.

Manager listens to reports from delegates

Delegate details latest progress

CHECKING ▶ PROGRESS
When delegates are actively involved in every stage of the process, and managers encourage them to share their views, delegation is a two-way system making the best use of everyone's skills.

MINIMIZING RISKS

Understanding the risks involved in delegating a task will help you to anticipate problems and monitor progress. So form contingency plans, take action to reduce risks, and intervene in good time before minor problems lead to major failure.

57 Ensure that bad news is not kept from you by a worried delegate.

MONITORING RISKS

When monitoring a delegate's progress, keep an eye on those areas of the task that you consider to be of high risk. For example, you may delegate the control of customer credit limits. Here, there is a risk of too high a level of credit being given to customers whose credit history is either unknown to you or who have been late payers in the past. This task will therefore require much more careful and consistent monitoring than a lower risk task, such as the maintenance of office equipment. Keep a list of all risks, and periodically check whether any of them can be eliminated.

58 Never gamble when taking risks: act on judgments based on probabilities.

USING MANAGEMENT BY EXCEPTION

Management by exception is a highly effective control method whereby a delegate informs their manager only of those exceptional events that require major decisions. You should not expect to hear about actions that proceed as planned, only of deviations from the plan. For example, a sales executive is asked to handle key accounts. As long as sales targets and profit margins are maintained, the delegator need not be involved in decisions. But if a customer suddenly asks for a higher discount, with a resulting drop in margins, the delegate must seek a decision from the manager.

59 Try to anticipate problem areas for the delegate.

60 Make contingency plans just in case things go wrong.

BUILDING IN CONTROLS

Key controls, such as a scheduled timeframe or specific budgetary limits, can be used as efficient constraints to guide and monitor a delegate. If tasks start missing deadlines or overrunning on cost, you must talk to the delegate immediately in order to identify the root causes of the problem as soon as possible. Ask the delegate to supply you with regular reports, both written and verbal, to gauge whether your initial brief was at fault or if the failures or deficiencies are a result of poor performance by the delegate. If the brief is at fault, revise it at once. If the problem lies with the delegate, consider providing further training or, if necessary, reassign the task to another delegate.

THINGS TO DO

1. List all possible risks in order of importance.
2. If possible, reduce a risk at the briefing stage.
3. Monitor all risks during the delegation.
4. Deal with the root cause of problems quickly.
5. Have contingency plans ready for immediate implementation.

61 Speedily remove delegates who make several serious mistakes.

TAKING FAIL-SAFE ACTION

In order to ensure achievement of the objective stated in the brief, it is prudent to build in an alternative course of action in case events do not follow expectations. For example, you may be using a bright but inexperienced delegate to maintain sufficient stock levels to keep one of your most important customers regularly supplied with a particular item. Here, you can minimize risk by ensuring that contingent stock is always available if the delegate under-orders or if the customer increases the units ordered unexpectedly.

CASE STUDY

Jane was marketing manager at a company producing garden furniture. Directors had set tolerance levels for customer complaints and returns at 3.5 per cent. This margin was accepted and planned for, and it was agreed that any increase should be brought to the attention of the marketing director.

When Jane became aware of a rise in returns, she suspected a problem at the factory. As instructed, she informed her superior, who then discussed the problem with his opposite number in production. It transpired that some of the machinery was worn out, but the finance department had vetoed its replacement.

The directors assessed the situation and decided that profit losses from returns would quickly outweigh the cost of new equipment, and ordered immediate purchase.

◄ **REDUCING RISK**
Here, the risk of the level of returns becoming too high is eradicated by setting a strict limit beyond which the matter is referred to a director.

REINFORCING A DELEGATE'S ROLE

When appointing delegates, always introduce them to team members, clearly stating the delegates' responsibilities. This will help delegates feel part of a team and encourage them to accept ownership of the tasks for which they are responsible.

62 Give praise when delegates notably improve on their performance.

INTRODUCING A ▼ NEW DELEGATE

Introduce a new delegate to existing team members, and inform any customers or suppliers who need to know the relevant responsibilities the delegate will have.

ESTABLISHING DELEGATES

For delegation to be effective, the delegator must always make a new appointment known. Having delegated a task, ensure that all relevant people who may be affected, including all colleagues, customers, and suppliers, are informed. If the appointment is high profile, make an occasion of the announcement – so boosting the delegate's prestige, pride, and confidence. Ensure that the exact nature of a delegate's responsibility is fully understood by all as confusion could be counterproductive.

Manager introduces new delegate

New delegate uses open body language

ACCEPTING IDEAS

When you delegate a task you are also delegating the right to make decisions. Openly encouraging delegates to use their own initiative at all stages of a task or project will give them an added interest in the task and will boost their self-confidence. Unless there are good reasons for not doing so, accept ideas even if you consider the benefits to be marginal. Demonstrating openness to others' ideas will also motivate all members of a team.

63 Treat delegates as equals when meeting with third parties.

64 Take action to get delegates to come forward with new ideas.

DELEGATING OWNERSHIP

The highest form of delegation is the transference of "ownership" of an entire project to a trusted individual. However, this delegation of ownership should extend to all delegated tasks, small or large, as it is one of the most effective of all incentives. You will encourage ownership by allowing delegates to plan and execute a task in their own way, and by suggesting that delegates find their own solutions to problems that arise.

COMPARING MANAGEMENT TECHNIQUES

UNDERMINING OWNERSHIP

COUNTERMANDING
The manager asks what decision has been made, or what action has been taken, and countermands the decision or action.

INTERFERING
The manager demands to be informed of any progress, expressing approval or disapproval, and does not allow the delegate ownership.

TAKING OVER
The manager does not trust the delegate, or is unable to relinquish control, and reclaims the day-to-day performance of the task.

REINFORCING OWNERSHIP

HANDS-OFF
The manager does not interfere during the performance of a delegated task, but is fully informed to ensure good execution.

ADVICE AND CONSENT
The manager takes on the role of an adviser to the delegate. Major decisions on issues raised by the delegate are agreed jointly.

COACHING
The manager uses the delegated task as an opportunity to develop delegates' skills and broaden their range of experience.

Providing Support

Delegates will often need positive support and encouragement in the early stages of an assignment. You can help them to succeed by providing all the information, time, and resources they need, and by being prepared to secure extra help if necessary.

65 Be aware that a helpful attitude may be perceived as interference.

Assessing Progress

It is a good idea to schedule meetings with your delegate before they embark on an assignment. If you are firm about deadlines and checks in the first place, you will be able to maintain regular contact and avoid the risk of your input being seen as an intrusion. Make it clear that you are available between those dates, and that you expect to be informed if any difficulties arise. When results deviate from expectations, examine the problem together from every angle, to find out whether it stems from a lack of resources, time, supervision, experience, or effort. You will then know what to do to put things back on course.

66 Meet at regular times for feedback sessions, but not too frequently.

Checking Progress with Delegates

When discussing progress with delegates, always use positive questions, like those below, that will encourage delegates to suggest their own solutions to problems. Avoid questions that may discourage or demoralize the delegate.

❝ Is there anything you want to bring to my notice? ❞

❝ We failed to meet that deadline. Any suggestions as to how that happened? ❞

❝ I see that costs are over-running. What steps are you taking to bring them back in line? ❞

❝ How do you think we can avoid making this mistake again? ❞

CONTRIBUTING ADVICE

Throughout the monitoring process, make it clear to delegates when you expect to be told about problems, and when not. The safest policy is to encourage them to seek advice when in doubt. If they fail to do this, problems may arise that could have been avoided. Always be sympathetic and encouraging when delegates ask for help, but be firm in delivering your verdict if you think the delegate could have dealt with the issue unaided.

67 Turn to members of staff whose work impressed you in the past.

SUPPLYING ASSISTANCE

At some stage your delegate may claim that he or she needs help from others in order to meet the task objective. Use your judgment to establish whether this is a legitimate claim. Then, with your delegate, work out how much assistance is needed and for how long. If no other staff are available, consider outside sources of help. Keep the names of qualified people to hand, but do not call on them too readily. Commit extra resources only if the project is at risk. Always try to keep to the brief that was agreed at the outset.

68 Consider using outside sources of help if necessary.

UTILIZING CONTACTS ▼
Keep an up-to-date list of experienced contacts ready to hand so that you can quickly find help when required.

Manager quickly locates known and trusted contact

Details of contacts kept on desktop index card system

MAINTAINING THE BOUNDARIES

When monitoring progress, ensure that the boundary between yourself and the task remains clear. Your delegate is now responsible for doing the work. If there are difficulties, the line may have to be crossed, but you should step back as soon as possible.

69 Having delegated a task, do not interfere with how it is done.

70 If you have to take back a task, start looking for a new delegate at once.

STEPPING BACK

As a delegation proceeds, you should gradually reduce the frequency of review meetings. This is especially the case when dealing with first-time delegates who may require more intensive supervision at the outset. Meeting very frequently defeats the object of delegation and reduces the delegate's, and your, available time. Never refuse a request for a meeting, but make it clear to the delegate that the aim is self-management.

ENCOURAGING SOLUTIONS

When a delegate runs into difficulties, it could give you great satisfaction to "magic" the problem away. But unless he or she learns how to deal with similar situations in the future, no progress is being made. Discourage delegates from arriving at your door before thinking an issue through. Instead, ask them to consider why the situation may have arisen, and insist that anyone coming to you with a problem should also come with two solutions and a stated preference between them. In this way, delegates will get used to working out solutions themselves and never form the habit of relying on you to come up with all the answers.

QUESTIONS TO ASK YOURSELF

Q Do I avoid interfering unless absolutely necessary?

Q Am I keeping the number of meetings to a minimum?

Q If a delegate is struggling, am I inclined to complete the task for them to save time?

Q Do I express confidence in my delegate in words and actions?

Q Do I encourage my delegates to work independently of me, and find their own solutions?

IDENTIFYING PROBLEMS

When an otherwise competent delegate leaves aspects of a task incomplete, look for the possible causes. Are you checking, interfering, or worrying too much, or even taking work back because you are dissatisfied? If your behaviour is the cause of the trouble, make changes immediately. If the problem lies with the delegate, consider all the possible causes. It could be that the delegate is overwhelmed by responsibility, is lacking in confidence, or is not coping well with criticism. Restate why they were appointed, reassert your confidence in them, and stress that criticism can identify opportunities to improve skills.

71 Keep all review sessions brief and well organized.

72 Do not let a delegate become discouraged when problems arise.

DIFFICULTIES WITH MAINTAINING BOUNDARIES

TYPICAL PROBLEMS	POSSIBLE SOLUTIONS
CONTINUAL INTERRUPTIONS You are continually asked questions and have to make decisions.	The delegate may mistakenly believe that everything must be double-checked by you. Explain that you expect them to act on their own initiative whenever possible.
DELEGATED TASKS REBOUND The delegated tasks, or parts of them, reappear on your desk.	Consider whether the task as a whole may be altogether too complex. Go through it with the delegate to see if it can be broken down into more manageable elements.
EXCESSIVE WORKLOAD Although you have delegated all you can, your workload has increased.	Over time you may have reclaimed small elements of many delegations, so your work consists of a series of unrelated tasks. Ensure that delegates retain complete tasks.
GIVING TOO MUCH SUPPORT You help out in order to save time and eliminate the risk of mistakes.	This could be a genuine misdelegation. Consider whether, for this particular assignment, you may have overestimated the abilities of your delegate, and act accordingly.
INSECURE DELEGATES You are constantly asked to check progress and give your approval.	Your delegate may feel intimidated by the responsibilities involved in completing the task. Overcome their anxieties by stressing your own confidence in their abilities.

GIVING FEEDBACK

The most effective way to review staff performance is to provide delegates with constructive feedback sessions after each task. Use these meetings to recognize and analyze achievements, and to discuss problems and solutions. But be sure to avoid laying blame.

BEING POSITIVE

One-to-one review meetings between delegator and delegate can achieve either constructive or negative results. To establish a positive environment, treat the session as a discussion between partners: air and discuss problems openly, and acknowledge achievements readily. Unless it is necessary, do not use the meeting to assert your authority, and ensure that any criticisms of the delegate's work are as constructive as possible with a view to improving performance.

73 Make sure that review sessions are conducted in a constructive way.

74 Use positive and polite language when managing all delegates.

▼ DISCUSSING PROGRESS
When reviewing a delegate's performance, be positive both in your praise and in any criticism you provide. Use the meeting as an opportunity to encourage a delegate who may be experiencing difficulties with a particular assignment.

Delegate provides progress report

Manager chooses informal seating arrangement to put delegate at ease

REVIEWING PERFORMANCE

For a final performance review to be effective you should systematically work through a clearly established agenda. Look especially at whether the final objective has been achieved. Consider:

- Did the delegate encounter any problems that meant revising the initial brief?
- Were the task's allocated resources adequate?
- Was it necessary to take drastic action following poor handling by the delegate?

Even if no problems were encountered, consider and discuss whether there are any changes that could be made that would improve general performance and efficiency in the future.

QUESTIONS TO ASK YOURSELF

Q Am I adopting a positive and helpful attitude during review meetings?

Q Is the delegate presenting me with all the essential facts?

Q Am I encouraging delegates to provide their own solutions?

Q Do I avoid allocating blame when mistakes occur?

Q Am I using review sessions to develop delegates?

AVOIDING BLAME

75 Hold impromptu review sessions only when it is really necessary.

From time to time, events will not proceed as planned: projects will go over budget, schedules will not be kept, or a particular task will have to be done again. When things go wrong, avoid the temptation to apportion blame – this may discourage the delegate. Instead, use a feedback session to analyze what has gone wrong to ensure that lessons are learned and that similar mistakes are avoided in the future.

OFFERING FEEDBACK TO YOUR MANAGER

When reporting on progress to your manager, try to be selective about the information you offer. There is little need to report back on every single aspect of a task. Your manager should neither need nor want to know every detail in order to assess your progress. If you are presenting either verbal or written information, report only on essential developments. Avoid the temptation to exaggerate those aspects that are going well, or to gloss over what is going wrong. If you have encountered problems or difficulties you wish to discuss, explain the causes, and state what action you propose to take. End the meeting by asking whether you have covered every issue of concern to your manager.

PRAISING AND REWARDING

Always acknowledge a delegate's exceptional performance, and give credit where credit is due. Identify all faults and errors, but remember that praise and reward play an important part in motivating and encouraging future achievements.

76 Use handwritten notes rather than typed letters to praise delegates.

THANKING A TEAM

When a task or project is successfully completed, an effective manager ensures that all the delegates who contributed to its success are duly and fairly credited. A delegator who takes little interest in a task and then assumes the majority of the credit is guilty not only of bad management, but also of bad manners. If you are presenting the finished task, consider involving your colleagues, and stress the contributions made by all members of the team.

PRAISING PUBLICLY ▼
Choose an appropriate time when team members are together to thank a specific delegate for exceptional performance.

Manager thanks delegate for his contribution to project

Delegate

Team members attend meeting

RECOGNIZING EFFORT

Never take satisfactory performance of a delegated task for granted – you will probably have set the delegate a reasonably stretching task. To achieve ambitious objectives, the delegate probably had to overcome several difficulties and cope with unforeseen events. He or she may have had to work long hours and will certainly have learned much during the assignment. Show that you are fully aware of what has been achieved and of the effort required, even if you also have to draw attention to various errors and omissions. Remember that pride in achievement is a prime motivator – perhaps the most important of all. Recognizing that achievement will help to ensure that a delegate's good performance continues.

CULTURAL DIFFERENCES

Reward practices vary greatly worldwide. In Japan, for example, exceptional performance is regarded as part of an employee's commitment to the job and is not rewarded separately. In the US and the UK, and increasingly in the rest of Europe, payments based on performance (with bonus payments for special achievements) are becoming much more common.

77 Always recognize the effort that was put into a task, and reward it.

PRAISING DELEGATES

The most effective way to praise a delegate is either in person or by letter – both methods will have a major motivational impact. Equally, failure to praise tends to undermine confidence rapidly. Remember that praise will be most welcome from a fair and honest critic, so do not devalue praise by using it excessively. Rewards in the form of salary increases, bonus payments, and non-financial benefits will all reinforce praise.

REWARDING EXCELLENCE

Delegates who excel in the performance of a task should always be appropriately acknowledged and rewarded. Any reward scheme you set up should recognize really exceptional performance with an appropriate reward, and should stimulate an expectation of future performance-based rewards. However, do not give special rewards to delegates who perform to expectation – that was part of the initial agreement when taking on the task.

78 When things have gone wrong, look for solutions – not scapegoats.

Analyzing Difficulties

Both the delegator and delegate need to analyze, and learn from, any difficulties encountered during a delegation. The first step towards finding a solution to a problem is to ascertain whether it stems from you, your delegate, the task brief, or procedure.

79 Try to give a delegate another chance if a task is mishandled.

Questions to Ask Yourself

Q Was I too hasty in making the appointment?

Q Is there somebody available who would do better?

Q How can I prevent this problem from recurring?

Q What would I do differently if I could start again?

Q What are the delegate's proven strengths and weaknesses?

Questioning Yourself

If a delegated task has not been performed to your satisfaction, look first at your own actions. Perhaps you should have kept this particular task yourself, or been more selective when choosing the delegate. Go over the brief to find out if you could have made it clearer, and examine your monitoring procedures to be sure that they were adequate for the task. Maybe you made yourself too remote, or did not provide sufficient guidance when problems arose. Be as objective as possible in this self-examination so that you can identify and deal with your own weaknesses.

Reassessing a Delegate

If your delegate is not performing as well as you expected, examine why and how you made the selection in the first place. If you systematically matched the needs of the task with available staff, then either the system, the task specification, or your assessment of the person is at fault – maybe a combination of all three. A delegate's failure may not necessarily mean that your choice was wrong – your own mistakes or circumstances beyond your control could be hindering the work. Do not let the issue drag on: discuss the matter with your delegate promptly, then take action. Consider reallocating a task only as a last resort.

80 Analyze your own actions if difficult problems arise.

81 Consider all the implications before you radically alter an agreed brief.

Revising a Brief

As a task progresses, discuss the brief and make any minor alterations at regular review sessions. If major difficulties reveal serious defects, consider whether a more rigorous monitoring process could have highlighted the problem sooner, or if a sudden change in circumstances has invalidated some of the brief's assumptions. Think carefully before you implement any changes, since an alteration of plans at this stage could solve one problem while creating several more. If the brief requires revision, remember that any really radical changes may require the choice of a new delegate.

THINGS TO DO

1. Look at your own role.

2. Consider whether the brief or the delegate is at fault.

3. Replace a delegate if absolutely necessary.

4. Review problems regularly.

5. Deal with any known difficulties at once.

Looking at Performance

Results alone will not necessarily tell you all you need to know about the performance of a task. More accurate indicators can be gathered from your feedback sessions with the delegate, and other personal observations. However, remember that you cannot maintain a delegate's trust if you make inquiries behind his or her back. Be open about seeking relevant information from trusted colleagues and inviting comments from those who are affected by the delegation. If any defects come to light, it is your responsibility to take steps to improve the delegate's performance.

82 Be open and constructive when discussing the performance of a task with a delegate.

Handling Difficulties with a Delegated Task

Understanding the process of delegation will help when you are the delegate, rather than the delegator. When matters do not proceed as planned you have a chance to show your initiative and resolution. Analyze the causes of problems, and take corrective action if you can – and keep your manager fully informed throughout. If correction is beyond your reach, say so at once, and work with your manager to find a solution. Remember that the successful outcome of a task is all-important and is the major factor by which your performance will be judged.

Rectifying Problems

As a manager, you must be able to identify and help to rectify any errors a delegate makes while undertaking an assignment. When a delegate makes a mistake and you have to make criticisms, phrase these tactfully and positively, addressing the actual problem rather than castigating the delegate. This positive guidance will encourage the delegate and help to prevent the same or similar errors from happening again.

83 Be firm with delegates who conceal errors or do not admit them.

84 Use mistakes as learning tools to improve your managerial skills.

85 Consider whether a project brief was the cause of any serious error.

Learning from Failure

Knowing how to deal with failure may be as valuable as the successful outcome of the task. Take the opportunity when things go wrong to extract as many useful lessons as possible. Naturally, managers and delegates alike will be tempted to come up with excuses rather than explanations when a failure occurs, but excuses elucidate very little and are usually smokescreens that obscure the real causes of error. When you have identified a failure, carefully analyze the causes and discuss these with the delegate. Always stress that the sin is not to fail but to make the same mistake twice.

CORRECTING ▶
PROCEDURES

In this case study the account supervisor's error was certainly avoidable and should not have occurred. However, the mistake offered the managing director a useful opportunity to pinpoint weaknesses in procedures and to change working methods.

CASE STUDY

When the Smith Printing Company lost money after underquoting a client's job, the managing director's first concern was to find out how such a mistake could have been made. The account supervisor admitted that she had failed to notice that the cost of folding and binding had not been included in the estimate. She had been working on other projects at the time and had been under pressure, but was otherwise unable to account for the oversight. It was essential to identify the factors that had led to the error, so time was spent looking at procedures. It emerged that in the estimate, folding and binding was simply listed as "finishing" and the client had been charged only for trimming. To avoid future errors, it was agreed that all future quotations should include a more specific breakdown of each job.

REVIEWING PROJECTS

An "action review" is a systematic approach to identifying and correcting mistakes. It involves regularly comparing actual progress made against the objectives in a brief. This allows you to analyze and explain deviations from the intended plan of action. Keep a record of the lessons learned from failures and successes so that you can revise procedures and provide a report for the benefit of other managers and delegates.

86 Keep notes of errors made and lessons learned for future reference.

ASSESSING DIFFICULTIES IN A PROJECT

ASPECTS OF PROJECT	FACTORS TO CONSIDER
OBJECTIVES The goal of a project, and interim targets that should be met.	● The long-term objective may not be reached if the initial brief was faulty and needs constant amendment. ● A project can flounder if interim targets are missed.
RESOURCES The people, finances, information, and equipment required.	● If in doubt, it is wise to overestimate the costs involved in a project to cover any unforeseen expenses. ● Inadequate facilities will impede even very able staff.
TIMESCALE The planned schedule for completion of the project.	● The risk of running over schedule can be minimized by detailing when each stage is to be completed. ● Unexpected problems can undo the best-laid plans.
METHOD The strategy for achieving a project's ultimate objective.	● To reach the desired outcome you must have a clear vision of the route you will take to get there. ● If initial plans alter, methods may also have to change.
AUTHORITY The responsibility for the decisions relating to a project.	● An inadequate level of autonomy for delegates hinders decision-making and can lead to avoidable delays. ● If authority is withheld, staff will be demotivated.
FEEDBACK The essential communication between delegator and delegate.	● A project that is in difficulty will fail unless there is a structured process of communication in place. ● Body language can reinforce or contradict your words.

ASSESSING YOUR ABILITY

Delegation requires a broad range of managerial abilities, from communication skills to the use of monitoring systems. Evaluate your performance by responding to the following statements, and mark the options that are closest to your experience. Be as honest as you can: if your answer is "never", mark Option 1; if it is "always", mark Option 4; and so on. Add your scores together, and refer to the Analysis to see how you scored. Use your answers to identify which areas need improving.

OPTIONS

1 Never

2 Occasionally

3 Frequently

4 Always

1 I trust people to work effectively, because I appointed them to do so.

1   2   3   4

2 I ensure that I have enough time for planning, training, and coaching.

1   2   3   4

3 I am loyal to my staff, and I expect them to show the same loyalty to me.

1   2   3   4

4 I monitor the progress of my delegates but without constant intervention.

1   2   3   4

5 I give my staff full and frank information wherever possible.

1   2   3   4

6 I try to do only the work that must be done by me, and delegate the rest.

1   2   3   4

7 I prioritize and devote time to personnel management.

1 2 3 4

8 I take great care over the structuring and reviewing of delegation.

1 2 3 4

9 I treat my subordinates as equals when establishing the best course of action.

1 2 3 4

10 I ensure that delegates understand the extent of their accountability.

1 2 3 4

11 I ensure that there are no overlaps in responsibility between delegates.

1 2 3 4

12 I am able to appoint or replace delegates quickly when required.

1 2 3 4

13 I always evaluate staff by looking at both positive and negative aspects.

1 2 3 4

14 I appoint the best person for the job, irrespective of age, experience, or seniority.

1 2 3 4

15 I involve my delegate in the process of preparing a full and detailed brief.

1 2 3 4

16 I make sure that there is adequate back-up available for delegates when needed.

1 2 3 4

17 I encourage delegates to use their initiative when confronted with problems.

1 2 3 4

18 I do not reprimand someone who fails while trying something new.

1 2 3 4

19 I gauge all delegates' performance, concentrating on significant indicators.

1 2 3 4

20 I ensure that I provide positive feedback to my delegates at all times.

1 2 3 4

21 I see to it that processes are examined regularly and adapted if needed.

1 2 3 4

22 I always use an agenda when reviewing progress with a delegate or team.

1 2 3 4

23 I keep an up-to-date log of which tasks I have delegated, and to whom.

1 2 3 4

24 I make myself available to see my staff and deal with any problems they have.

1 2 3 4

25 I consider all possible alternatives before reclaiming a delegated task.

1 2 3 4

26 I make a special point of recognizing all outstanding achievements.

1 2 3 4

27 I make opportunities to thank delegates for all tasks successfully completed.

1   2   3   4

28 If I make a mistake, I accept the responsibility without making excuses.

1   2   3   4

29 I give the benefit of the doubt, but act quickly if a delegate must be replaced.

1   2   3   4

30 I analyze actions to find, and teach, the lessons of success and failure.

1   2   3   4

31 I ask for feedback from employees and react positively to what I learn.

1   2   3   4

32 I use any failures to learn valuable lessons for future delegations.

1   2   3   4

ANALYSIS

Now you have completed the assessment, add up your total score, and check your performance by reading the evaluation below. Identify your weakest areas, and refer to the relevant sections in this book to develop or refine your delegating skills.

32–63 You are not truly delegating, and what you are doing is ineffective. Strive to make improvements immediately.

64–95 Some of your delegation is working very well, but there are obvious gaps in your performance that need to be rectified. Consider delegating more tasks, and ensure that your delegates have enough freedom to carry out their assignments.

96–128 You are an effective delegator and are likely to be receiving positive feedback. Identify and improve on the weaker aspects of your performance: 128 out of 128 is the aim.

IMPROVING SKILLS

The process of delegation provides an ideal opportunity to raise skill levels in your staff and in yourself. Use it to assess staff and motivate them at all levels.

DEVELOPING DELEGATES

To allow delegates to develop their skills, you need to offer them support and help. These include making available the resources and facilities for staff to be trained on a continuous basis, setting achievable targets, and providing effective appraisals.

87 Train your staff so that they can undertake a variety of tasks.

88 Set an example to your staff by being trained yourself.

89 Try not to underestimate a delegate's qualities.

COMBINING TASKS

By broadening a delegate's skills, you can appoint that delegate to handle a complete task whose individual elements would previously have been done by a number of people. For example, the financing of customer purchases at one company was split between five people and took seven working days to complete. It was calculated that most of this time was spent handing the project between staff who also had higher priority work to finish first. A decision was taken to allocate the whole task to one person backed up by a specialist team. The completion time was cut to four hours.

TRAINING STAFF

It is ineffective and demoralizing to delegate a task to someone who lacks the necessary skills. Never place people in new or changed roles without first providing the training they need, and always keep the option of further training available. Ask suitably skilled delegates too if there are any areas that need developing – this can be highly motivational. Always build delegation on a foundation of on-going training at all levels so that suitably qualified people will be available whenever you need them.

▲ **CHOOSING A TRAINING PROGRAMME**
Consider budgeting for a certain amount of staff training each year. Compare course details, and remember that the cheapest training programme may be a false economy in the long term.

REASSESSING ABILITIES

Delegating a task will give you the opportunity to assess a delegate's abilities. If the delegate has worked for you before, you will have a chance to reassess his or her performance in the light of any new demands and challenges.

Always keep delegates' performances under constant review, since new tasks are likely to reveal either hidden talents or areas in which deficiencies become apparent. Reassessment of delegates sometimes reveals that a staff member is being used for tasks that are far beneath his or her potential abilities.

▼ **TRAINING TO COMMUNICATE**
When the director realized that problems in the workshop were the result of poor communications, he initiated a training programme for one of his key staff.

CASE STUDY

The efficiency and reputation of a major vehicle service centre was being weakened by interdepartmental resentment. When promises were made to customers that could not be fulfilled, the counter and the workshop staff blamed each other. To build an understanding between the two teams, the director decided to develop workshop manager Ryan's communication skills and give him an opportunity to work with the counter staff. Ryan was then able to demonstrate some of the shop-front issues to staff in the workshop, and vice versa. When required, he was also able to assist in situations where customers had technical inquiries.

Being in contact with the whole job gave Ryan great satisfaction. Customers benefited from his specialist knowledge, and the conflict between the teams ended.

COACHING DELEGATES

When delegating, a manager takes on the role of a coach, talking to staff and encouraging their development. One of the most important points to discuss with delegates is whether they are tackling tasks in the most efficient way. Delegates who are keen to impress may not wish to ask for help, so ensure that they are working within their skill levels. If they are not, provide the appropriate training or back-up to improve their abilities.

> **90** Set aside some of your working week for coaching your key delegates.

Display shows structure of project

Delegate notes down information

Manager explains developments

▲ FINDING TIME TO DEVELOP STAFF

Consider setting aside some regular time every week to keep your staff informed of any new developments and to concentrate on developing skills in the specific areas in which you are keen to delegate work.

SETTING TARGETS

One of the most effective ways of developing delegates is through setting targets. However, set targets at levels that both you and the delegate consider attainable through good performance. This will enable both of you to anticipate and focus on areas of the task in which the delegate's skills need to improve. This type of on-the-job training will help the delegate to complete the task and move on to more difficult ones.

BEATING EXPECTATIONS

Staff can exceed expectations if you set them ambitious but achievable targets and let them make their own decisions about how to attain them. This hands-off approach has two major benefits: delegates are motivated by being given the freedom to use their initiative and improve their own performance, and the organization as a whole benefits through the improved efficiency demonstrated by the newly motivated workforce.

91 If people appear dissatisfied by the reward system, find out why.

DO'S AND DON'TS

✔ Do ensure that employees are aware that training is available if needed.

✔ Do thank those who have performed well.

✔ Do tell delegates that they should ask others for help when needed.

✔ Do ask people what additional skills they feel they require.

✔ Do encourage delegates to use their own initiative to achieve objectives.

✘ Don't forget that financial reward is not always the most effective motivator.

✘ Don't stifle creativity by emphasizing rules over results.

✘ Don't assume that all criticism is always discouraging.

✘ Don't set obscure targets that could seem unattainable.

✘ Don't neglect a delegate who may be struggling with a task.

PRAISING EFFECTIVELY

Deliver praise to a delegate as soon as possible after the occasion that merits it. Be genuinely warm, but not effusive, and be specific about the aspects you have most admired. Comparisons are sometimes beneficial: if the delegate has outshone others in certain ways, make that a point of admiration. The object of praise is to thank and to motivate, and thus to establish a foundation on which to build still-better performance.

OFFERING REWARDS

People are paid for meeting expectations, so avoid incentive schemes that pay bonuses for expected performance. Remember that the delegator and the delegate share the same goals. You want the job to be done well, and they want to do the job well. Their earnings are likely to improve as they continue to develop their skills. So try to ensure that performance meets or exceeds expectations, and reward exceptional performance separately.

92 Set realistic targets, and be flexible in case events force a change of plan.

APPOINTING SUB-LEADERS

The development of sub-leaders is a major part of a manager's task. This involves encouraging the appointment of deputies, sharing authority by promoting the most qualified candidates, and considering all means of training for potential leaders.

93 Ask a senior to keep an eye on a deputy when you are absent.

DEVELOPING DEPUTIES

As a manager it is important for you to assess your staff continually for potential sub-leaders. Remember that there will be times when you are absent and someone will have to deputize for you. Delegation to cover your absence, or to take over part of your work temporarily, will provide an opportunity for potential future leaders to step into your shoes. Develop reliable deputies by deputizing as much and as often as you can. This will free you to concentrate on high-level tasks.

94 When appointing a deputy, announce it to your staff with confidence.

DELEGATING AUTHORITY

You, as leader, are ultimately responsible for appointing or removing sub-leaders, altering instructions, or changing levels of responsibility. However, the more authority that you give your sub-leaders to exercise on delegated tasks, the more they will develop their own skills – including those of delegation. Always encourage sub-leaders to follow your example and share as much authority as possible with their own delegates.

Expertise in communication

Commitment to the task

A steady temperament

Loyalty to the organization

A confident manner

▲ **WHAT TO LOOK FOR IN A SUB-LEADER**
When selecting a person for a leadership position, consider all the qualities that a potential candidate will bring to the role. Look for relevant experience and reliability combined with excellent communication skills, confidence, and enthusiasm.

POINTS TO REMEMBER

- Delegated leaders should be given the opportunity to prove their worth to their colleagues.

- Sharing authority does not mean giving it away. The manager always remains ultimately responsible.

- Trusted deputies should be given the freedom and discretion to do jobs in their own way.

- Leadership training is vital for the person concerned as it will teach them to manage subordinates.

- Character as well as professional knowledge plays a part in the making of a successful leader.

PROMOTING ON MERIT

To avoid negative reactions following a promotion to a leadership position, you must be careful to choose your candidate solely on the grounds of merit. People who are promoted beyond their capabilities will feel inadequate, and their insecurity will make them less effective. Others, especially those who have been passed over, may feel that they have been unfairly treated and will be demotivated. Even with a deserved promotion, the attributes that you have recognized may not be immediately appreciated by others. So show that you have confidence in your delegate/sub-leader as the right person for the job. A genuinely deserving delegate will not take long to fulfil your expectations and justify his or her appointment.

PROVIDING TRAINING IN LEADERSHIP

There are plenty of leadership courses from which to choose, and effective ones will teach specific skills and reinforce the personal characteristics and expertise needed by a sub-leader. Leadership training is often run in combination with other programmes, such as quality management. However, learning the theory of management is not enough. Leadership is an interpersonal skill and has to be practised in a real environment. So consider providing opportunities for subordinates occasionally to lead a team. The role need not be permanent, nor need it depend on status. Rotating the leadership of task forces or similar sub-groups is an excellent means of showing people, through their own experiences, what the requirements of leadership are.

▲ DEVELOPING LEADERS

Management training can take place away from the workplace. Outdoor activity courses will assess and develop team-working and leadership abilities.

DEVELOPING YOURSELF THROUGH DELEGATION

You should never become so busy developing others through delegation that you neglect your own development. While the delegating process is an education in itself and will free your time, it can be reinforced through formal instruction.

95 Organize sufficient time in which to research and develop new ideas.

96 Set yourself a weekly or monthly reading plan and try to stick to it.

IMPROVING PERFORMANCE

Delegation involves some of the most important aspects of the manager's job: selection, planning, and operating through others to achieve results. These activities are such an intrinsic part of the management process that the delegator is able to improve his or her efficiency simply by delegating well. But good performance can always be better. There is no absolute level of attainment, even in settled conditions. To be a successful manager you must undergo routine self-assessment, and look for ways to develop new and improved skills.

REASSESSING TASKS

As you develop your delegating skills, your staff will naturally progress, improving and increasing their own skills and gaining in confidence and experience. Reassign those individuals who have outgrown their initial task, and are ready to take on more, or higher-level, work. Also, monitor the performance of your team as a whole, to assess whether they are capable of undertaking higher-profile projects. This will improve the structure and balance of your workload, allowing you to take on other tasks and achieve still better results.

QUESTIONS TO ASK YOURSELF

Q Am I up-to-date with current management issues?

Q Have I become complacent about my own performance?

Q Do I invest enough time in looking for new ways to deal with familiar problems?

Q When I am guiding others, how often do I stop to listen to my own advice?

DEVELOPING YOUR SKILLS

Use the delegation process to free yourself from structured work, such as administration, so that you can undertake more demanding and unstructured tasks, such as managing people, solving problems, and researching new ideas. It is by constantly developing these special skills that you as a manager can raise your performance from the adequate to the exceptional.

97 If you are aware of a gap in your management education, fill it.

UTILIZING TRAINING

Seek relevant training even if you feel you have reached the top. Consider taking advantage of courses that teach skills that you have not yet mastered in order to increase your area of expertise, or use them to update your knowledge and develop new ideas. Remember that many trainers and approaches are available to meet your own specific needs, so your options are limitless.

98 Reinforce your skills by taking the opportunity to learn from others.

EDUCATING YOURSELF

A pizza multimillionaire in the US has the world's biggest library of self-help books. Whether or not the books contributed to his success, the principle is powerful. Every one of those books contains ideas or techniques designed to make the manager's job easier and improve performance. Although managers acquire knowledge and know-how as they carry out their tasks and communicate with others, there is much to be gained from an organized approach to self-education. Take time to study and absorb books, journals, and other media, and the pay-off will be incalculable.

▼ STUDY TO SUCCEED

Make use of distance learning if you cannot spare the time during the day or evening to attend a "live" course.

Take notes of important points

DEVELOPING YOUR BOSS

Although you may have developed effective delegation skills, your own manager's approach to delegating tasks to you may be deficient. Ask yourself if this is because your manager has not fully understood your abilities, or is it because he or she feels threatened by you? Consider saying to your manager that you feel underused and are able to take on more responsibilities. Adapt your manner to the situation, and always be polite.

99 Develop the habit of speaking frankly to your manager at all times.

MANAGING YOUR CAREER

When planning your career, actively seek ways to make progress – do not wait for your advance to be dictated by events. Use your delegating skills to give yourself time to think about your aims and ambitions. Consider writing a career plan, complete with target dates, for advancing from one stage to the next. Working towards these targets will give you a positive attitude that will help you to identify and make the best of any career opportunities that arise.

John is promoted to project leader and is introduced to members of his team

John's poor delegation skills rapidly lead to inefficiency, and delays

▲ MAKING PROGRESS BY DELEGATING

This manager realizes that his underuse of delegation adversely affects his performance. Improving his delegating skills enables him to use his time more productively, develop and pursue a career plan, and achieve promotion.

BEING PROACTIVE

In today's fast-changing world, managers are expected to be highly independent and proactive. Showing initiative, making up one's own mind, and taking charge of one's destiny are all qualities valued by organizations who recognize that they need managers with these skills to survive in a competitive climate with fast-moving markets. To be effective, managers must be able to act rather than react under pressure, and delegate efficiently. So strive to stretch yourself and use your abilities to the full in your present position, and look for and seize any chances to exercise responsibility. If the organization denies you the opportunity to develop, the best response may be to move on.

100 Ask where you want to be in ten years time, and plan your route.

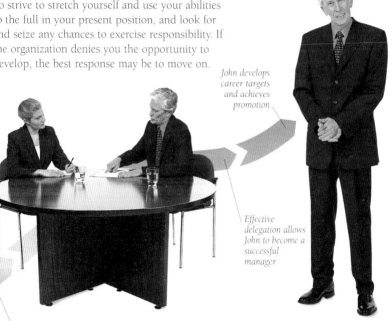

John develops career targets and achieves promotion

Effective delegation allows John to become a successful manager

Having taken steps to improve his delegating skills, John starts using his team members much more productively

101 Do not keep quiet about your ambitions – let your superiors know what you want to achieve.

INDEX

ACKNOWLEDGMENTS

AUTHOR'S ACKNOWLEDGMENTS

This book owes its existence to the perceptive inspiration of Stephanie Jackson and Nigel Duffield at Dorling Kindersley; and I owe more than I can say to the expertise and enthusiasm of Jane Simmonds and all the editorial and design staff who worked on the project. I am also greatly indebted to the many colleagues, friends, and other management luminaries on whose wisdom and information I have drawn.

PUBLISHER'S ACKNOWLEDGMENTS

Dorling Kindersley would like to thank Jayne Jones and Emma Lawson for their valuable part in the planning and development of this series, everyone who generously lent props for the photoshoots, and the following for their help and participation:

Editorial Christopher Gordon, David Tombesi-Walton; **Design** Austin Barlow, Kate Poole; **DTP assistance** Rachel Symons; **Consultants** Josephine Bryan, Jane Lyle; **Indexer** Hilary Bird; **Proofreader** Helen Partington; **Photography** Steve Gorton; **Photographer's assistant** Sarah Ashun; **Photographic co-ordinator** Laura Watson.

Models Philip Argent, Angela Cameron, Kuo Kang Chen, Roberto Costa, Patrick Dobbs, Vosjava Fahkro, Ben Glickman, Richard Hill, Zahid Malik, Maggie Mant, Sotiris Melioumis, Frankie Mayers, Mutsumi Niwa, Lynne Staff, Daniel Stevens, Gilbert Wu, Wendy Yun; **Make-up** Elizabeth Burrage, Lynne Maningley.

Special thanks to the following for their help throughout the series:
Ron and Chris at Clark Davis & Co. Ltd for stationery and furniture supplies; Pam Bennett and the staff at Jones Bootmakers, Covent Garden, for the loan of footwear; Alan Pfaff and the staff at Moss Bros, Covent Garden, for the loan of the men's suits; David Bailey for his help and time; Graham Preston and the staff at Staverton for their time and space.

Suppliers Austin Reed, Church & Co., Compaq, David Clulow Opticians, Elonex, Escada, Filofax, Gateway 2000, Mucci Bags.

Picture researchers Victoria Peel, Sam Ruston; **Picture librarian** Sue Hadley.

PICTURE CREDITS

Key: *a* above, *b* bottom, *c* centre, *l* left, *r* right, *t* top
Ace Photo Library: Jigsaw 2 4–5; **Pictor International, London** 61*tr*; **Telegraph Colour Library** 66*bl*; **Tony Stone Images**: Sean Arbabi 65*br*. Front cover **Ace Photo Library**: Jigsaw 2 *cla*.

AUTHOR'S BIOGRAPHY

Robert Heller is a leading authority in the world of management consultancy and was the founding editor of Britain's top management magazine, *Management Today*. He is much in demand as a conference speaker in Europe, North and South America, and the Far East. As editorial director of Haymarket Publishing Group, Robert Heller supervised the launch of several highly successful magazines such as *Campaign*, *Computing*, and *Accountancy Age*. His many acclaimed – and worldwide best-selling – books include *The Naked Manager*, *Culture Shock*, *The Age of the Common Millionaire*, *The Way to Win* (with Will Carling), *The Complete Guide to Modern Management*, and, his latest book, *In Search of European Excellence*.